DIESELS AND SEMAPHORES

Roger Siviter ARPS

Oxford Publishing Compa

Plate 1 (Title page): Class 31/1 No. 31166 enters Leicester (London Road) Station with the 15.25 service from Birmingham (New Street) to Cambridge on 2nd July 1983.

Plate 2 (above): English Electric Class 40 No. 40197 approaches Scarborough with a special excursion from Rhyl on 14th August 1983. Framing the scene is an LNER three doll bracket signal, with miniature arms for slow speed movements to and from running lines; the arms are mounted on wooden posts.

INTRODUCTION AND ACKNOWLEGEMENTS

When British Railways finally changed its motive power from steam to diesel and electric traction in the 1960s, it could be considered the greatest single change that had taken place on our rail network — certainly in this century. Because of this change, several main lines (notably the West Coast route) and many secondary lines were completely altered in character. Stations were rebuilt and modernised, many steam sheds were closed and demolished and a host of modernisation schemes took place. Couple this with the Beeching closures of around the same period when many dozens of branch lines were closed, and a great many goods sheds and sidings were demolished on the existing network, and we have a picture of a very considerably altered railway scene; and so many of the things of the past had gone forever, with one notable exception — the semaphore signal.

Although this method of signalling did not dominate the network it was still there on many main lines and secondary routes notably, in the West of England and East Anglia, to name but two areas. But in the last few years this has begun to change and many resignalling schemes are now in progress which will mean that in the not too distant future the semaphore signal will be a thing of the past. This of course means not only the signals, which in themselves are visually very colourful and attractive, but many splendid signal boxes (some dating from pre-grouping days) will also inevitably disappear with the advent of the modern power box.

This book sets out to show the modern diesel locomotives and trains set against this background, and give us a visual record of scenes that will soon become history. For help and assistance in this I am greatly indebted to many railwaymen of all grades and also to J. Gordon Blears for a great deal of technical help and information, and to Joan Wappett for all the typing, and last but not least, to my wife, Christina, for all the help she has given me in the preparation of this book.

From a technical point of view, all the pictures were taken with Nikon cameras and lenses using a wide variety of lenses from 35mm to 200mm. The film stock used was Ilford XP1 developed in XP1 chemicals.

R. Siviter
October 1984

Copyright © 1985 Oxford Publishing Co.

ISBN 0-86093-345-8

Typesetting by:
Aquarius Typesetting Services, New Milton, Hants.

Printed in Great Britain by:
Balding + Mansell Ltd., Wisbech, Cambs.

Published by:
Oxford Publishing Co.
Link House
West Street
POOLE, Dorset

Plate 4 (above): The 17.07 Paddington to Hereford train, hauled by Class 50 No. 50041 *Bulwark*, prepares to leave Worcester (Shrub Hill) Station on 15th June 1983. The signal is a GWR type bracket signal.

Plate 3 (Introduction page): The 12.29 Lincoln to Crewe service passes a fine example of a North Staffordshire Railway signal box at Alsager, on the Stoke to Crewe section of its journey, on 9th June 1984.

Plate 5 (History page): Evening at Skipton, on 4th November 1983, as Class 45/1 'Peak' No. 45146 prepares to leave with the 16.35 Carlisle to Leeds train. Skipton contains a mixture of LMS and BR type signals, the signal on the left being of the latter type.

HISTORY

The early railway pioneers had much more to think about than developing the steam locomotive for the newly emerging iron railways of the 1830s, since the steam railway was a totally new transport concept. Never before had man travelled at more than the speed of the horse and never before had man travelled on a guided way in which the vehicles had to follow a fixed line of rails. Although railways of one type or another had been known since the 16th century for mine and quarry use, wih timber baulks providing the bed and the guiding influence on hand pushed or horse drawn barrows or wagons, speeds were low and provided that there was some operating discipline the men and horses followed each other with their loads at no more than walking pace. If one tripped up then the others behind could see what was amiss and would stop, unless they were not looking where they were going. But the steam railway was different; speeds were much higher — 30, 40 and more miles an hour, loads were heavier, but the primitive hand brakes on engines and coaches were hardly effective for the job, and trains often took a mile in which to stop. Certainly the railway pioneers had made the trains go but they had not provided them with the means to stop quickly. The powerful air-operated disc brakes of today would take more than a century to be developed. Thus it was quickly realised that some form of signalling would be needed on the early steam railways, to tell engine drivers whether they could proceed or whether they must stop.

With nothing to go on it was left to each railway to decide just what form the signals should take. Some relied on hand signals given by the duty policemen employed at each station or junction (here the railways took as their example the then recently formed Metropolitan Police in London, responsible for law and order, and traffic control) while on some railways the police used flags, and lamps by night. There were varieties of fixed board signal with discs, squares, rectangles, even flags in frames hoisted to the top of a pole. The indications differed from railway to railway; on some, a board face-on to a train meant stop, in others it meant carry-on. Most suffered from the fact that they gave only one indication positively, since the other indication was sometimes given with the board edge-on to the driver and thus not visible until in close proximity. If a signal blew down in a gale there was no real cer-

tainty that it was missing if say, in the clear position, the board was edge-on and unseen anyway. The Great Western Railway provided quite distinctive indications for danger and clear by having a crossbar face-on to a train for danger, and a disc at right angles to it which when face-on meant clear, the whole assembly rotating through 90 degrees so that one or other could always be seen.

Another form of signal already in established use for communication across country was the semaphore which, by different angles of a pivoted rectangular arm, was used to pass messages from one hilltop observation post to the next. In 1841 the London & Croydon Railway chose the semaphore for use as a railway signal, and other companies soon followed. In the railway application, the arm which operated on the left of a slotted post, from a pivot within the slot, had only three positions and meanings: horizontal — danger, stop; inclined down at 45 degrees — caution, slow down; and hanging vertically within the post — clear, proceed. The indications were used in conjunction with the then method of train operation known as the time interval system.

Although the electric telegraph had been developed around the time when the first railways were opened, and indeed the Great Western installed a trial section, its use for sending messages about train movements was not appreciated. Thus trains followed one another on minimum time limits controlled by the station police. Once a train had left a station a danger signal would have been displayed behind it for five minutes. Then the signal was placed in the caution position for a further five minutes before it was finally set at clear. This assumed that the first train was proceeding on its way, for there was no way of telling if a train had broken down until the guard went back towards a station to warn a following train, or the policeman at the station, if no following train was encountered. The time interval varied by a few minutes from line to line. Thus the semaphore, as it was first used on railways, was a three-position signal and lasted in that form for 30 to 40 years on some lines. At night, oil lamps with coloured glasses working in conjunction with the arms gave the indications, red — danger, green — caution and white — clear.

Once the benefits of the electric telegraph were realised, and it had become reliable, it was installed on a

few lines from the 1850s between stations and signal boxes to allow messages to be sent as a train passed, so that a space interval, rather than a time interval, was provided between trains. The section of line between two signal boxes became known as a block section and not more than one train was allowed to occupy that section on one line at a time. As a train entered and left, its movement was reported on the block telegraph by the signalmen, as they were now called, from one signal box to the next. Thus there was no longer any need for semaphore signals to show three indications since the block section was either clear or occupied; there were no half measures. The semaphore signal became a two-position signal, horizontal for danger and inclined down at 45 degrees for clear, with red and white lights at night.

The change came gradually as railways, often reluctantly, adopted the block system, but it was finally imposed by law in the 1889 Regulation of Railways Act. In the following decade, as gas lighting became more widespread for street and house lighting, clearly, confusion could arise with the semaphore signal white light, the night time clear indication. As there was no longer any use for a caution indication in its original form, green became the colour to denote clear, proceed.

Even with the introduction of power braking by the vacuum or compressed air systems, trains of the 1890s were heavier and faster and still needed about one-half to three quarters of a mile in which to stop from their top speeds. Thus distant signals were provided at about this distance from a signal box to give advanced warning to a driver of the indications shown by the stop signals ahead. Semaphore signal arms by this time had taken on the form familiar today, with the stop arm painted red on the front face, with a white vertical stripe near the left-hand end, and the red and green spectacle at the right-hand end for the night time indications. Sometimes the green glass was in fact blue, which showed green with the yellow flame of the oil lamp behind it. Distant signals at that time were also painted red but with a fishtail 'vee' notch cut out of the left-hand end and a white 'vee' or vertical stripe near the left end. At that time, too, distant signals showed red or green lights at night, even though the horizontal position and the red light denoted caution; the signal could be passed in the horizontal position but with the driver preparing to slow down and stop at the signals ahead.

In British signalling the semaphore arms at junctions showed which route a train was to take, and if there were three possible routes ahead, then the driver would be faced with three semaphore arms arranged geographically from left to right and the arm in the clear position showed the route set for the train. Usually the signal applying to the line with the highest speed was higher than the others although, in some cases, it was the most important route which was the highest, which might not have been the fastest track. Major junctions such as Newcastle, York, Rugby and terminal stations like St. Pancras, with multi-track approaches, had massive gantries with 20, 30 or more arms spanning the tracks, and drivers had to be very careful to identify the signal which applied to them.

Through the years of World War I there was little change in British signalling and the semaphore was the standard type throughout Britain and Ireland, though with detail differences in design. Spectacle shapes varied from railway to railway, although the products from signalling contracting firms in private industry were often distinctive, being seen on several railways. Arms varied by an inch or so in length and width, and for confined locations were often short and squat.

In the early 1920s two developments radically altered the style of semaphore signals in Britain, following experiments by one or two companies around World War I. The three-position semaphore had made a re-appearance in a few isolated installations, but this time the arm worked in the upper quadrant; that is upwards from the horizontal danger position. Inclined up at 45 degrees with a yellow light at night denoted caution — be prepared to find the next signal at danger, and vertically upright with a green light at night meant line clear, proceed. The aim was to provide stop and distant indications in one arm where successive signals were spaced fairly evenly at ½ to ¾ of a mile intervals. The form of signal had been derived from American practice, although there, the arm was to the right of the post. However the three-position semaphore was not adopted widely, and in the early 1920s signal engineers agreed that where multi-indication signals were required, they should be of the colour-light type and no further three-position semaphores were installed; although one or two lasted until the 1950s.

However the decision not to put in any more three-position signals, left the way open for upper-quadrant two-position semaphores which could be lighter and with smaller balance weights than were needed for lower quadrant semaphores, to ensure that the arm returned to danger, particularly if the operating wire broke. From then on, the upper quadrant semaphore became the new standard on three of the four main line railways of the Grouping period from the 1920s until nationalisation in 1948. Only the Great Western resisted the change and continued with lower quadrant signals; even after nationalisation its Western Region successor persisted with the same policy so that today, lower quadrant signals can be seen in many parts of the Western Region and on former GWR routes where mechanical signalling has not yet been replaced by power operation and colour-light signals. On the other three railways the upper quadrant type gradually replaced older lower quadrants, but as on the Western, colour-light signals now control long lengths of principal main lines.

The second change of the 1920s was an alteration to distant signals which, from then on, were painted yellow, with a black 'vee' stripe corresponding to the 'vee' notch cut out of the left-hand end. At night they showed yellow or green lights. Both lower and upper quadrant distants were altered to the new colour over several years.

Today, semaphore signals survive on most secondary routes and a few principal main lines, although change is coming. They outlasted the steam age and even the first of the diesel years. Today, Inter-City 125 High Speed Trains are controlled by semaphores on some routes, though not at their top speeds. Although the change to modern signalling is proceeding apace, it seems likely that the semaphore signal, with its long history, will just about last into the next century.

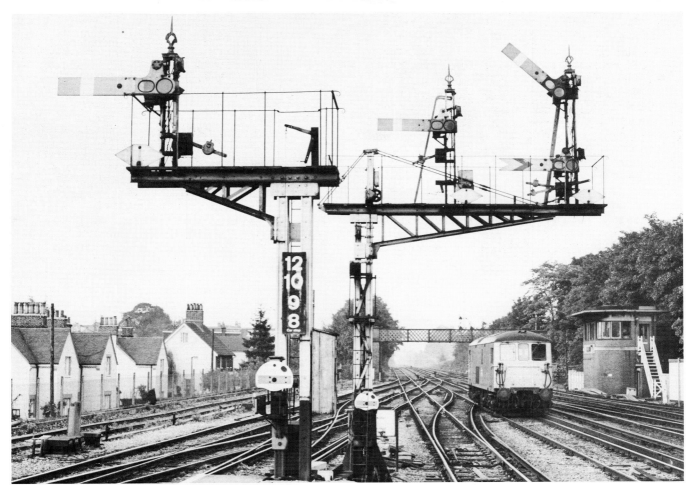

Plate 6 (above): A Class 73 electro-diesel locomotive, No. 73126, pulls away from Redhill and heads north on 1st September 1983. These signals are a good example of Southern Railway rail-built bracket signals complete with Southern disc signals. The modern looking box on the right is of typical pre-war Southern Railway design.

Plate 7 (below): Tunbridge Wells (West) is the location as Class 207 East Sussex Unit No. 1319 enters on 31st August 1983 with the 09.37 Eridge to Tonbridge working. The train is framed by a Southern Railway gantry, and the ornate lattice posts and finials are worthy of note. The signal box is LBSCR.

Plate 8 (above): Framed by a typical BR bracket signal at Aynho Junction, on 24th October 1983, is an unidentified Class 47 locomotive hauling a southbound merry-go-round train. Note the GWR style lower quadrant signal on the down line, a reminder of the past on this former GWR (later Western Region) main line from Paddington to Birmingham (Snow Hill).

Plate 9 (right): Class 33/0 No. 33011 leaves Blatchbridge Junction near Frome, on 7th May 1984, and heads down the West of England main line with an e.c.s. train. Overlooking the scene is a GWR home signal, and Blatchbridge Junction box is seen in the background.

Plate 10 (above): A Holyhead to Llandudno afternoon local train is framed by an LMS gantry with BR type tubular post dolls as it approaches Llandudno Station on 18th June 1982. The bracket signal is also of the LMS type and the signal box is pure LNWR, built around the turn of the century.

Plate 11 (below): Class 37 No. 37059 leaves the yard at March (South) Junction, on 25th July 1983, with an eastbound tank train and passes an LNER bracket signal.

Plate 12 (above): On a glorious summer evening in 1983 (20th June) the 17.07 Paddington to Hereford train, hauled by Class 50 No. 50046 *Ajax*, drifts down the bank between Worcester (Shrub Hill) and Foregate Street Station. To the left of the railwaymen coming off duty from Worcester Depot, a GWR type bracket signal, which guards the junction of the London and Foregate Street—Birmingham lines can be seen.

Plate 13 (below): Conway is the setting as Class 47/4 No. 47502 gets the 'all clear' from a BR upper quadrant signal and heads for Holyhead, with the 17.34 from Crewe, on 18th June 1983.

Plate 14: On 16th July 1983 Class 40 No. 40129 pulls out of Spalding with the 14.34 (SO) Yarmouth to Manchester (Piccadilly), and approaches the remains of an ex-LNER lattice post signal, which has been modified by a standard BR tubular post home and distant signal. This summer (Saturdays only) working was regularly in the hands of English Electric Class 40 locomotives.

Plate 15: Class 47/0 No. 47052 is surrounded by a fine array of LNER signals as it accelerates out of Ely, on the evening of 22nd July 1983, with the 19.04 King's Lynn to Cambridge train. The LNER signal box completes the scene.

Plate 16: On 16th July 1983 Class 47/0 No. 47026 approaches Havenhouse with the 15.35 (SO) Skegness to Peterborough train. The two home signals protecting the crossing are fine examples of GNR somersault signals with concrete posts.

Plate 17 (above): Passing the splendid GWR signal box at Truro, on the evening of 30th May 1984, is Class 47/4 No. 47560 *Tamar* with the 15.00 Plymouth to Penzance train. Completing the scene is a GWR home signal, situated at the end of the 'up' platform.

Plate 18 (below): This typical GWR gantry, situated at the western end of Exeter (St. David's) Station, has been a familiar landmark for several years but it is soon to be replaced by colour light signalling. On 28th April 1984 it provides a frame for Class 45/1 'Peak' No. 45126 with a Birmingham to Paignton extra. On the left Class 33/0 No. 33038 is waiting to leave with the 12.20 service to Waterloo.

Plate 19 (above): Helsby Junction, situated roughly halfway between Warrington and Chester on the ex-Birkenhead Joint line, is the location as English Electric Type 4 No. 40096 hurries through with a Trafford Park to Holyhead Freightliner train on the evening of 15th April 1983. The line to the right goes to Hooton and Birkenhead, and the impressive signals are BR standard home **repeating type.**

Plate 20 (below): Also pictured at Helsby Junction on the same evening is Class 47/4 No. 47577 *Benjamin Gimbert GC* with a Bangor to Manchester train. Note the smart appearance of the locomotive with its silver roof and black indicator panel.

Plate 21 (above): A signalman's view of Class 47/0 No. 47013, on 20th August 1983, as it approaches Elgin with the 14.48 Inverness to Aberdeen.

Plate 22 (right): Class 37 No. 37022 passes a North British bracket signal post as it enters Crianlarich on a misty summer morning, 19th August 1983, at the head of the 09.19 Fort William to Glasgow train. The line to Oban swings away to the left beyond the bracket signal.

Plate 23 (above): Passing a post-grouping GWR bracket signal (with route indicator apparatus) at Dovey Junction on 13th August 1983, are Class 25 locomotives Nos. 25181 and 25220 with the summer (Saturdays only) 07.00 Shrewsbury to Aberystwyth service. The area around Dovey Junction has many different types of GWR signals, although the standard BR pattern upper quadrant signals are beginning to replace them.

Plate 24 (below): Class 45 'Peak' No. 45023 The Royal Pioneer Corps coasts past Falsgrave signal box at Scarborough, on 14th August 1983, with the 08.00 (SuO) from Manchester Victoria. The area around gantry is NER with LNER type dolls and fittings.

Plate 25 (left): The 13.30 Bradford (Forster Square) to Keighley working is seen approaching Shipley on 4th November 1983. The signal box is of Midland Railway design, and the bracket signal is early LMS. The ornate station panelling is worthy of note. The line swinging away to the left is to Ilkley and Leeds.

Plate 27 (right): A Class 47/4, No. 47463, passes through Hellifield on Sunday, 15th April 1984, with the diverted 10.05 Manchester to Glasgow train. The fine looking signals have Midland Railway wooden posts but with LMS replacement fittings, and the finials have been removed.

Plate 26 (left): Shipley Station again, on the same afternoon, only from the reverse direction. The train about to depart is the 14.00 Keighley to Bradford (Forster Square). At the foot of the bracket signal is a pair of ground signals, and also worthy of note are the very fine station buildings and the splendid chimney pots.

Plate 28 (right): Also on the same day, the diverted 11.10 Glasgow to Euston train leaves Hellifield hauled by Class 47/4 No. 47434. The signal box is pure Midland Railway.

Plate 29: This view taken trom Dingwall signal box, on 20th August 1983, shows Class 37 No. 37017 approaching with a special from Aberdeen to Kyle of Lochalsh. The signal in the background is an early LMS design bracket signal.

Plate 30: A busy scene at Inverness, on 20th August 1983, as Class 08 No. 08717 shunts the empty stock of a Wick train, and Class 37 No. 37261 prepares to leave with the 10.45 to Kyle of Lochalsh service. There are contrasting signals here, with a BR type on the left and a Highland Railway signal post with LMS attachments on the right.

Plate 31: Class 33/1 No. 33119 arrives at East Grinstead on 30th August 1983 with the 17.34 train from London Bridge. Framing the train are typical short posted Southern Railway signals built from old bullhead rail; a common practice on the Southern Railway.

Plate 32 (above): Haydon Bridge Station, complete with North Eastern signal box and LNER signal, is the setting for Class 37 No. 37106 hauling a Carlisle to Newcastle train of flat wagons on 16th August 1983.

Plate 33 (below): Token exchange at Bedale, on 17th April 1984, as Class 47/0 No. 47291 approaches the North Eastern signal box with the daily Redmire to Tees Yard hoppers. The box controls the station as well as the crossing on the busy A684 Northallerton — Hawes road which is a link from the A1 road to the M6 motorway.

Plate 34 (right): Another shot of the previous train, (No. 47291) this time at Ainderby near Northallerton. The signals controlling the crossing are LNER and the box is North Eastern Railway.

Plate 35 (below): Another North Eastern Railway signal box, this time the splendid example at Haltwhistle on the Newcastle to Carlisle line. The train is a Carlisle to Newcastle coal empties hauled by Class 37 No. 37106 on 15th August 1983. Note the staggered platform layout and the very fine footbridge.

Plate 36: Class 33 locomotives Nos. 33106 and 33030 are pictured as they work 'light' out of Westbury Station after bringing in a stone train from the west, on 26th May 1983. By this date the colour light signals are in place by the side of the GWR lower quadrant semaphores, in readiness for the completion of the Westbury power box.

Plate 37: Class 50 No. 50046 *Ajax* glows in the evening sunshine, on 30th July 1983, as it pulls past the splendid gantry of Western Region lower quadrant signals at Newton Abbot with a Plymouth train. Note also the GWR signal box of wooden construction.

Plate 38 (below): The 11.05 Weymouth to Westbury local leaves Frome on 7th May 1984, and pulls away under this interesting GWR bracket signal complete with centre-balanced arms.

Plate 39 (right): A picturesque scene at Alsager, on 9th June 1984, on the former North Staffordshire Railway line from Crewe to Stoke-on-Trent. The train pulling out of the station is the 11.20 Crewe to Lincoln (St. Mark's). This bracket signal, containing BR home, distant and siding semaphores, is due for replacement by colour lights in the near future.

Plate 40 (above left): Passing a BR bracket signal at Blea Moor, on 21st April 1984, is Class 45/1 'Peak' No. 45142 with the 09.07 Leeds to Carlisle train.

Plate 41 (below left): Class 47/4 No. 47581 *Great Eastern* with the 15.30 Liverpool Street to Norwich train speeds past an LNER lattice post signal at Diss on 23rd July 1983.

Plate 42: This rare example of a Furness Railway signal post is to be found at Salthouse Junction, Barrow; note the very fine finial. The train is the 15.35 Barrow to Crewe working and is being hauled by Class 47/1 No. 47536.

Plate 43 (above): Accelerating past a typical GWR lower quadrant bracket signal at Lostwithiel, on 31st May 1984, is Class 47/4 No. 47567 in charge of the 08.27 Penzance to Paddington train, which is normally an HST service.

Plate 44 (below): Dalmally, on the former Caledonian route to Oban, is the setting for Class 37 No. 37192 (of Eastfield Depot) on 23rd August 1983 as it climbs into the station with the 12.25 Oban to Glasgow train. It is passing a beautiful Caledonian Railway home signal post, complete with a splendid

Plate 45: This GWR bracket signal at Worcester (Shrub Hill) stands guard over Class 37 No. 37129 as it performs some evening shunting duties on 15th June 1983.

Plate 46 (above): Class 45/1 'Peak' No. 45145 hurries through Taunton on 9th July 1983 with an 'up' relief train. This gantry is a good example of post-1923 GWR signalling.

Plate 47 (below): The 13.24 (SO) Llandudno to Stoke train, consisting of three two-car units, is framed by an array of BR upper quadrant signals at Abergele on 4th June 1983. The signal on the left is pulley operated (quite rare) compared to the one on the right which is crank operated. The actual gantry and upright is probably of LMS design.

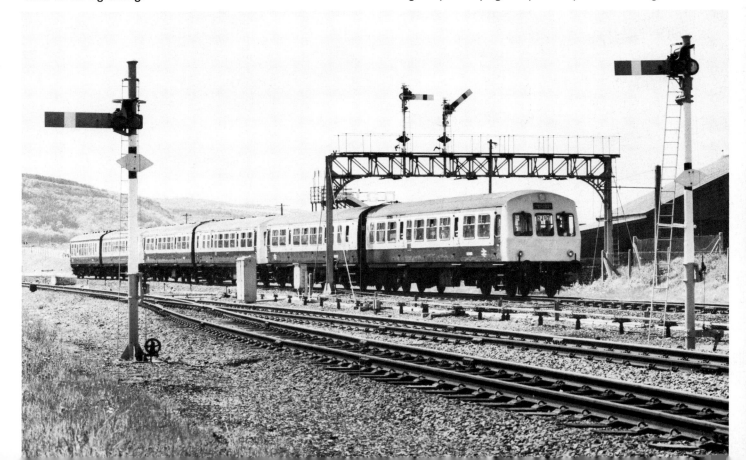

Plate 48 (left): Conversation piece at Westbury, on 26th May 1983, as the crew of Class 47/0 No. 47287 find time for a quick word with one of the signalmen at Westbury box. With the completion of the new power box, this splendid box has, sadly, since been demolished.

Plate 49 (above): Class 47/4 No. 47406 *Rail Riders* hauls the 07.05 Edinburgh—Newcastle—Carlisle train on 16th August 1983 and is framed by the edge of the former NER box at Haltwhistle, and the dual direction LNER bracket signal with two homes (one for the Alston branch). Until recently, Haltwhistle was the junction for this branch, the remains of which can be seen disappearing to the right of the train.

Plate 50 (above): East Grinstead, in the heart of commuter land, is the setting for Class 33/1 No. 33119 as it waits to enter the station on 30th August 1983, with the stock for the 18.46 working to London Bridge. Completing the scene is an LBSCR signal box and a Southern Railway short post rail-built signal.

Plate 51 (left): On the last day of August 1983, Class 33/0 No. 33058 is seen approaching Uckfield with the 17.20 train from London Bridge. Note the LBSCR signal box complete with wheel for opening and closing the crossing gates, the edge of which can be seen in the left foreground.

Plate 52 (above): The driver of the 19.50 local service to Plymouth gets a cheery wave from the signalman as No. L425, a Class 117 Pressed Steel Co. Unit, pulls out of Liskeard on 27th April 1984. The line to the left leads to the platform for Looe branch trains. This fascinating signal is of the GWR inverted bracket centre-balanced type. Note the GWR ground disc signal raised to a higher level, and the GWR signal box.

Plate 53 (right): Token exchange at St. Dennis Junction (Newquay branch), on the evening of 30th May 1984. The train is the 19.55 Par to Newquay service. St. Dennis was once the junction for the line to Burngullow (on the Penzance—Plymouth line) and the branch line to Meledor Mill. A typical GWR lower quadrant signal gives the 'all clear' for the unit to proceed to Newquay.

Plate 54: Class 25 No. 25035 and Class 31 No. 31102 are pictured at Blea Moor, (on the Settle—Carlisle route) on 5th November 1983, with the 'Cumbrian Mountain Pullman'. The signal is a BR upper quadrant with miniature arm for controlling the loop lines.

Plate 55 (facing page): The line ahead is clear as Class 47/0 No. 47234 rounds the curve into Lostwithiel on a beautiful spring evening, 27th April 1984, with an 'up' china clay train.

Plate 56:   The 09.32 Par to Newquay train climbs out of St. Blazey on 27th April 1984. The Class 118 Birmingham RC&W unit, No. P464, approaches a latter day GWR lower quadrant signal, which originally would have had a wooden support post and not a tubular metal post, as shown here.

Plate 57 (right): 'Deltic' locomotive No. 55016 *Gordon Highlander* pulls under the NER box mounted on Selby swing bridge, on 24th May 1981, with the 11.43 York to Kings Cross train.

Plate 58 (below): This elegant GWR balance bracket signal guards the entrance to the western end of Exeter (St. David's) Station. The train is the 09.32 Penzance to Paddington and is hauled by Class 50 No. 50048 *Dauntless* on 26th May 1984. A feature of this signal is that the distant arm on the middle post is motor driven, the other two being fixed distants. Framed between the gantry and the train is a fine example of a GWR box, which is shortly to be made redundant on completion of the power box but, happily this box is destined to be preserved by a group of enthusiasts. On the left hand side of the picture another Class 50 locomotive waits to leave on a midday Waterloo train. Finally, in this interesting scene, note the pair of GWR elevated ground signals by the bracket posts.

Plate 59 (left): On 18th February 1984, Class 33/0 locomotive No. 33020 is seen approaching Church Stretton with the 13.25 Crewe to Cardiff train. There is a mixture of GWR lower and BR upper quadrant signals in this scene, plus a GWR box.

Plate 60 (right): On 4th June 1983, Class 45/1 locomotive No. 45103 passes a pair of LMS bracket signals and approaches a banner repeater signal at Abergele. The train is the 15.40 Manchester (Victoria) to Bangor working.

Plate 61 (below): Class 45/1 'Peak' No. 45115 hurries past the Midland Railway signal box at Finedon Road, Wellingborough with a Newcastle to Eastbourne special on 14th May 1983.

Plate 62 (above): Class 20 locomotives Nos. 20178 and 20172 pass the Midland Railway signal box at Leicester (North) on 2nd July 1983 and approach Leicester (London Road) Station with the 12.37 service from Skegness. In the right background is the depot, and locomotives on shed that day included 46028, 31204, 47525 and a rare visitor, Class 40 No. 40015, which had worked in the previous evening on a parcel train. Semaphore signalling still dominates this area but it is shortly due for modernisation.

Plate 63 (left): GWR type lower quadrant signals form the background on 1st July 1983, as Class 37 No. 37224 is involved in shunting coal wagons at Droitwich.

Plate 64 (above): Class 40 No. 40057 approaches Pelham Street Crossing, Lincoln, with a return Cleethorpes to Shrewsbury excursion on 25th July 1983. In the background is an LNER bracket signal.

Plate 65 (below): Class 31 locomotives Nos. 31316 and 31154 haul the 09.35 Norwich to Birmingham train and leave Leicester (London Road) Station on 9th July 1983. On the left a 'down' London HST service is about to enter the station, the frontage of which can be seen at the top of the picture. On the gantry is a selection of modern home and distant signals.

Plate 66: Class 25 No. 25161 passes an LMS left hand bracket signal as it takes the Barrow line out of Carnforth, on 29th September 1983, with a down ballast train.

Plate 67: An immaculate Class 40, No. 40004, with 'The Broadsman' from York—Ipswich—Lowestoft—Norwich—York, passes the line from Beccles as it heads through Oulton Broad (North) Junction on 24th July 1983 for Norwich and York. An LNER bracket signal controls the entry to the junction from the Lowestoft end.

Plate 68: The 17.45 Norwich to Liverpool Street train hurries through Stowmarket, on 23rd July 1983, hauled by Class 47/4 No. 47577 *Benjamin Gimbert GC* and passes the Great Eastern signal box and LNER repeater signal. Scenes like this will soon become a memory with the completion of the Eastern Region electrification scheme.

Plate 69: Class 47/0 No. 47085 *Mammoth* of Stratford Shed is framed by a variety of LNER signals as it approaches Ely on 23rd July 1983 with the 07.48 (SO) King's Lynn to Liverpool Street service. The fine box is of Great Eastern origin.

Plate 70: Class 33 No. 33062 sets off from Exeter (St. David's) Station with the 10.00 to Barnstaple train on Saturday, 30th July 1983, and is framed by a post-grouping GWR four doll bracket signal. One of the features of this signal is that the distant arm on the third post is motor driven, and another is that the distant arm on the fourth post is fixed. Note also the particularly fine finials on these signals.

Plate 71 (above): Class 26 locomotives Nos. 26024 and 26035 pull out of Dingwall on 20th August 1983, with the 11.40 Inverness to Wick train. Towering over the train is a Highland Railway bracket signal post with LMS attachments.

Plate 72 (left): Turning round we see the train at the junction of the Wick and Kyle lines, at the point where the token is handed over. In the distance is a pair of home and distant signals which guard the junction from the Kyle and Wick lines respectively.

Plate 73 *(above)*: Lincoln Cathedral dominates this late evening scene at Greetwell Junction on 25th July 1983, as Class 37 No. 37140 ambles past a pair of Great Northern bracket signals with LNER fittings on its way back to Lincoln.

Plate 74 *(below)*: Twilight at Ipswich, on 23rd July 1983, as Class 47/4 No. 47581 *Great Eastern* coasts into the station at the head of the 18.45 Norwich to Liverpool Street train. Framing the train is an array of LNER signals. As well as the Class 31 stabled in the yard, the former LNER coach on the right hand side, now probably used as a tool store is noteworthy.

Plate 75 (above): On 25th July 1983, Class 37 No. 37061 approaches Spalding with a southbound goods. Class 31 No. 31114 is seen shunting the sidings on the left hand side; the signals are of LNER design.

Plate 76 (left): Class 45/1 'Peak' No. 45129 speeds under an LMS bracket signal at Holywell Junction, North Wales, on 6th July 1983, with the 11.15 Bangor to Manchester (Victoria) train. A Class 25 locomotive waits in the loop with a 'down' ballast train.

Plate 77 (above): On 25th July 1983, Class 37 No. 37102 approaches the GER box at Downham Market with the 10.35 Liverpool Street to King's Lynn train. Completing the scene is an LNER bracket signal.

Plate 78 (below): Class 47/3 No. 47359 rounds the splendid LNWR Chester No. 2 box with a morning Holyhead to Crewe Freightliner train on 6th July 1983.

Plate 79: On 29th May 1984 Class 45/1 'Peak' No. 45128 leaves Totnes and starts the climb up Rattery Bank with the 12.02 Birmingham to Penzance train. As can be seen from this picture, work is under way to replace the GWR semaphores with colour light signals.

Plate 80 (above): Class 45/1 'Peak' No. 45150 approaches the LMS signal box at Appleby (North) with the 16.00 Leeds to Carlisle train on 20th April 1983.

Plate 81 (below): Cowley Bridge Junction on the evening of 30th July 1983. The train passing the fine pair of GWR bracket signals is the 17.05 Plymouth to Birmingham (New Street) hauled by Class 47/4 No. 47419.

Plate 82 (left): Weymouth is the setting as Class 47/0 No. 47287 pulls out of the station with a return excursion to Swindon, on the evening of 29th August 1983. The signal is of the Southern Railway style rail-built bracket type, complete with raised disc signals.

Plate 83 (below): A Machynlleth to Shrewsbury evening local train approaches Caersws on 12th August 1983. Noticeable is the mixture of lower and upper quadrant signals, a common sight in this area ever since the LMR took over from the WR some years ago.

Plate 84 (left): On the ex-GWR Wolverhampton to Shrewsbury line, at Cosford, during a wintry 25th January 1984, Class 45 'Peak' No. 45009 passes a modern upper quadrant signal while hauling a mixture of tanks and coal wagons bound for the south.

Plate 85 (left): On the same day, and same location, Class 25 No. 25207 heads north with coal empties and passes the former GWR signal box but, as in the previous scene, the signals are now of the LMR upper quadrant type.

Plate 86 (right): Rood End Sidings, near Langley, on the former GWR Stourbridge Junction — Birmingham line, provides a wintry setting for Class 31 No. 31171 on the afternoon of 25th January 1984. The locomotive has just worked out of the siding on the right which runs into Allbright & Wilson's chemical works, and is shown in the right background. Once again, due to regional changes, there is a mixture of upper and lower quadrant signals.

Plate 87: Framed in the GWR gantry at the north-eastern end of Westbury Station on 26th May 1983, is Class 33 No. 33026 with the 15.10 Bristol to Portsmouth Harbour train. The lines on the right lead on to the West of England — Paddington main line.

Plate 88: An unidentified Class 47 heads for Banbury with the 09.14 Gatwick to Manchester (Piccadilly) service on 24th October 1983. Once again, because of regional changes, we have a mixture of modern upper quadrant signals and a GWR lower quadrant in use side by side.

Plate 89: Class 47/0 No. 47291 pulls through Bedale with a Redmire—Tees Yard hopper train on 16th April 1984. The wooden post bracket signal is LNER and the short signal is a North Eastern lattice post, but with a replacement finial.

Plate 90: On 17th April 1984, the 13.42 train from Middlesborough to Whitby is framed by a wooden post LNER two doll bracket signal on the approach to Battersby Junction, set in the North Yorkshire Moors. In the background are a further two LNER bracket signals but of all metal construction. These control the junction of the Middlesborough and Whitby lines, all trains needing to reverse at Battersby.

Plate 91 (above): The 17.44 local train, to Weymouth comprising Class 119 Gloucester RC&W unit, No. B590, approaches Castle Cary, on 7th May 1984, and passes a fine array of GWR lower quadrant signals which, sadly, are due for replacement by colour lights in the near future.

Plate 92 (right): A busy scene at Par, on 27th April 1984, as Class 37 No. 37185, hauling a 'down' china clay train, passes No. 37182 waiting to back on to a failed HST set in the station. In the background is a GWR two doll bracket signal, not an uncommon sight at the moment in this area.

Plate 93 (above): The grand old Victorian station at Tunbridge Wells (West) is the setting, as Class 207 'East Sussex' diesel electric unit No. 1317 pulls out and approaches a pair of Southern Railway rail-built signals with the 10.34 Eridge to Tonbridge service on 31st August 1983.

Plate 94 (below): Class 33/2 No. 33209 leaves Shrewsbury on 3rd July 1983 with the 13.36 (SuO) Crewe to Cardiff train. On the right is a GWR three doll bracket signal and the elegant abbey overlooks the scene.

Plate 95: Overlooked by a tower block of flats at Smethwick (West) on 14th April 1984 is Class 50 No. 50033 *Glorious* on a Plymouth–Witton football special. The train has just passed the former GWR box which controls the junction. Originally the WR trains ran on the line by the colour light (now a spur) which led to the main GWR Wolverhampton to Birmingham line (now closed) and so to Birmingham (Snow Hill) Station. The line in the foreground was mainly used for transfer traffic to and from the LMR.

Plate 96: This wooden post LMS signal still guards the Midland main line just south of Wellingborough as Class 47/4 No. 47484 *Isambard Kingdom Brunel* hurries through with the 16.25 St. Pancras to Derby train on 15th May 1983.

Plate 97: Class 40 No. 40096 has just passed a typical BR upper quadrant signal and forges towards Helsby Junction on the evening of 15th April 1983 with a Trafford Park — Holyhead Freightliner train.

Plate 98 (above): Class 45/1 'Peak' No. 45117 passes a wooden post LMS home and distant signal as it accelerates out of Wellingborough on 15th May 1983 with the 17.15 (SuO) St. Pancras—Derby train. The next day (16th) saw the start of the new timetable when nearly all the trains became HST workings, and many of the Class 45s were transferred to work on the North Wales route.

Plate 99 (below): Light and shade at Leicester (London Road) Station as a southbound HST departs for London on 2nd July 1983. The train is the 15.10 Nottingham to St. Pancras working. The signal at the end of the platform is a banner repeater.

Plate 100 (left): On 30th May 1984, Class 50 No. 50005 *Collingwood*, in charge of the 09.40 working from Paddington to Penzance, approaches St. Erth. The GWR two doll bracket signal frames the GWR signal box. St. Erth is the junction for the St. Ives branch which comes into the station at a separate platform, the start of which is concealed by the railings on the left.

Plate 101 (left): A GWR two doll bracket signal dominates the scene at Langley Green, in the West Midlands, as Class 50 No. 50033 *Glorious* approaches the station with a return football special from Witton to Plymouth, on 14th April 1984. The reason for the extreme difference in height of the two dolls is due to sighting from the other side of the station footbridge.

Plate 102 (right): The road ahead is clear for Class 50 No. 50042 *Triumph* as it pulls out of Taunton with the 09.02 Liverpool (Lime Street) to Penzance train on 11th April 1983.

Plate 103 (above): The 15.18 Cleethorpes to Newark train is framed by LNER bracket signals as it approaches the Great Central Railway signal box at Barnetby Junction on 26th July 1983. The train is hauled by Class 31/4 No. 31408.

Plate 104 (right): The 15.25 Birmingham to Ely train approaches Melton Mowbray on 15th July 1983 and is hauled by Class 31 No. 31145. The box is of LMS design and the reason for the overhang is for sighting purposes for the signalman.

Plate 105 (above): Class 47/4 No. 47478 passes a typical medium size LNWR box at Hednesford on the Rugeley—Walsall line with an up West Coast Main Line train diverted from the Trent Valley line on Sunday, 29th May 1983. The modern BR signal makes an interesting comparison with the signal box. Also in the background is an LMS style bracket signal.

Plate 106 (below): Passing the GER box at March, on 25th July 1983, is Class 31 No. 31102 with the 09.03 Cambridge to Birmingham train. This locomotive was one of the first of the class to be built, later locomotives having a headcode panel on the front of the roof. Note also the decorative barge boards on the signal box.

Plate 107 (above): Class 47/4 No. 47450, in charge of a Manchester to Plymouth train, is framed by this fine example of a GWR gantry at the eastern end of Newton Abbot Station on 12th April 1983. The dolls and support poles are of wooden construction as is the GWR signal box on the left-hand side.

Plate 108 (below): The sun is setting as Class 47/4 No. 47423 pulls out of Inverness and approaches Welsh's Bridge box with the 17.10 service to Edinburgh on 3rd October 1982. The gantry has a fine array of lattice post supported home, distant and calling on signals. The signal box is of Highland Railway design.

Plate 109 (above left): The mist and rain roll over the Highlands, on 23rd August 1983, as the 08.34 Glasgow to Fort William and Mallaig train, hauled by Class 37 No. 37027 *Loch Eil*, rolls into Bridge of Orchy and passes a typical modern upper quadrant bracket signal.

Plate 110 (left): A few minutes later No. 37112 (complete with yellow door panels) pulls out of Bridge of Orchy with the 09.19 Fort William, to Glasgow service and approaches another good example of a modern bracket signal.

Plate 111 (above): An unidentified Class 47 crosses the swing bridge at Trowse, Norwich, on 24th July 1983, with the 09.17 Norwich to Liverpool Street train and climbs past a rare example of an LNER lattice post, bearing signals for both directions of travel. This type of signal is used in confined areas, and is more often found on single track lines such as in colliery areas.

Plate 112 (above): The 15.45 Paignton—Exeter local, comprising Class 118 Birmingham RC&W unit No. P463, pauses at Newton Abbot on 27th May 1984. This wooden post GWR signal has home, distant and calling on arms. Note also the splendid station clocks, presented to the GWR by the people of Newton Abbot in 1927, on the occasion of the opening of the new station.

Plate 113 (right): The Southern Railway rail-built signal at Eggesford gives the 'right away' to the 18.45 Barnstaple to Exeter train on 26th May 1984.

Plate 114 (above): On 14th August 1983, Class 40 No. 40197 accelerates through Seamer (West) Junction with the return 'Whistler' railtour from Scarborough to Rhyl. It is framed by a fine pair of LNER bracket signals and NER signal box.

Plate 115 (left): Another Class 40, on this occasion No. 40080, is shown passing the GER signal box at Harling Road with the 15.11 (Saturdays only) Norwich to Manchester (Piccadilly) train on 6th August 1983. This train which started from Yarmouth, was regularly worked by Class 40s in the summer of 1983.

Plate 116: Class 26 No. 26012 poses by a Highland Railway lattice post bracket signal, with LMS fittings, at Inverness on 4th October 1982.

Plate 117: Class 40 No. 40168 hurries past the LNWR signal box at Abergele with a 'down' afternoon goods on 4th June 1983.

Plate 118 (above): On 20th August 1983, Class 37 No. 37183 coasts past this fine example of a Highland Railway bracket signal post (with LMS attachments) as it approaches Dingwall with the 11.10 Kyle of Lochalsh to Inverness train.

Plate 119 (right): A Class 205 'Hampshire' three car diesel electric unit, No. 1107, forms the 11.15 London Bridge to Uckfield service and approaches Eridge on 31st August 1983. The splendid lattice post bracket signal is of early Southern Railway design, and the box is LBSCR.

Plate 120 (above): Passing a fine array of wooden post signals at Finedon Road, north of Wellingborough, on 14th May 1983, is Class 45 'Peak' No. 45103 with a Nottingham to St. Pancras morning train. Note also the Class 45 in the goods loop.

Plate 121 (below): Stratford-based Class 47/4 No. 47585 County of Cambridgeshire is seen climbing out of Ipswich near Ipswich (East Suffolk) Junction with the 14.30 Liverpool Street to Norwich train on 5th August 1983. Both sets of signals are the LNER lattice post type, and the bracket signal on the left is the rarely seen gallows type. The imminent electrification of this main line will bring to an end such sights as this.

Plate 122 (above): An immaculate Class 47/4, No. 47581 *Great Eastern*, hurries past the Great Eastern box at Ipswich (East Suffolk) Junction with the 14.25 Norwich—Liverpool Street train on 5th August 1983.

Plate 123 (below): Class 37 No. 37193 shunts in the yard at Ipswich, on 5th August 1983, before leaving for Norwich with an afternoon goods. Note the LNER signals in the background.

Plate 124 (above): No. 03197, one of a diminishing number of Class 03 shunters, is pictured at Norwich on 17th August 1983 shunting empty stock. The LNER bracket signal also has route indicators and in the background is Norwich (Thorpe) signal box which is of GER design.

Plate 125 (below): Class 45/1 'Peak' No. 45137 The Bedfordshire and Hertfordshire Regiment (T.A.) approaches Skegness with the 09.22 (SO) train from Derby, on 16th July 1983. The signal box is of Great Northern origin but the bracket signals are of BR design and replaced GNR somersault signals some years ago.

Plate 126 (above): Class 33/0 No. 33062 approaches the GWR box at Cowley Bridge Junction, Exeter, with the 08.35 Barnstaple to Exeter (St. David's) train on 30th July 1983. In the foreground is the Paddington—West of England main line. The train is coming off the former Southern Railway route from Exeter to Plymouth which now only runs as far as Meldon Quarry. The Barnstaple branch diverges at Coleford Junction.

Plate 127 (left): A silvan setting in the heart of the Black Country as Class 50 No. 50010 *Monarch* climbs into Rowley Regis with a Plymouth—Witton 'Footex' on 14th April 1984. Because of regional changes, this former GWR line from Stourbridge Junction to Birmingham, now has a mixture of upper and lower quadrant signals. There were eleven football specials from Plymouth that day for the semi-final of the FA cup at Villa Park. Six ran via the Lickey Bank route and the other five via Worcester (Shrub Hill) and Stourbridge Junction. All five trains were hauled by Class 50s.

Plate 128 (above): GWR bracket signals abound in this portrait of Class 25s Nos. 25284 and 25276 as they hurry away from Dovey Junction, with the 09.45 (SO) Wolverhampton to Aberystwyth train on 13th August 1983. The hills towering in the background are part of the slopes leading up to the summit of Tarrenhendre (2,076ft.).

Plate 129 (right): On 21st January 1984, Class 33 No. 33029 approaches Aynho Junction with a southbound Freightliner. It is seen passing one of the few examples of lower quadrant signals still left on this former GWR Paddington to Birmingham main line.

Plate 130 (above): Class 50 No. 50035 *Ark Royal* gets the 'right of way' at Exeter (St. David's) Station and prepares to leave with the 12.20 to Waterloo on 26th April 1984. The train will take the route to the left of the picture, which is the start of the 1 in 37 up to Exeter (Central) Station (former Southern Railway), the tracks in the centre leading to Newton Abbot and Plymouth. This photograph shows the fine array of GWR signals etc. still to be seen at

Plate 131 (below): This is the view from the other end of the station and shows Class 50 No. 50006 *Neptune* waiting to leave with a Birmingham train, on 28th April 1984. Note the splendid GWR box which controls the eastern end of the station and goods yard beyond. Also notice the man just below the station sign who is on crossing duty — a very busy job, especially on summer Saturdays.

Plate 132 : A sign of the times as Class 37 No. 37100 is framed in the remains of a bracket signal on the approach to Shildon, on 16th April 1984, with a coal train bound for Bishop Auckland.

Plate 133 (above): Class 40 No. 40082 pulls out of Blackpool (North) on 17th September 1983 with the 09.46 to Stranraer. The box is L&Y and the signals are a mixture of LMS and BR.

Plate 134 (below): Class 47/0 No. 47106 approaches a Southern Railway rail-built three doll bracket signal at Exeter (Central) Station with the 11.10 from Waterloo, on 31st July 1983.

Plate 135: This fine GWR bracket signal still dominates the western end of Lostwithiel Station, on 27th April 1984, as Class 37 No. 37182, of Plymouth (Laira) Shed, approaches with an 'up' weedkiller train.

Plate 136: Class 37 No. 37261 approaches Dingwall with the 10.45 Inverness to Kyle of Lochalsh train on 20th August 1983. It is passing a fine example of a Highland Railway signal post with LMS attachments. The signal box at the rear of the train is also of Highland origin. Note also the former goods shed on the right.

Plate 137: Framed by this bracket signal at Dawlish Warren, on the morning of 28th April 1984, is an 'up' extra hauled by Class 47/0 No. 47249.

Plate 138: On a beautiful autumn day, 22nd October 1983, the 14.00 Shrewsbury to Chester local service pulls out of Wrexham (General) and passes a variety of GWR type signals. While the signal box on the right is GWR, the box on the left is Great Central; a reminder of pre-grouping days in this area.

Plate 139 (facing page): The Southern Railway bracket signal at Eridge receives attention on 31st August 1983.

Plate 140 (above left): Class 33/1 No. 33113 arrives at Exeter (Central) Station with the 08.37 from Waterloo on Saturday, 30th July 1983. Mounted on the left-hand side of the bridge is an early Southern Railway gallows or suspended doll type bracket signal.

Plate 141 (below left): A Stoke to Crewe local train approaches Alsager on the afternoon of Saturday, 9th June 1984. Apart from a BR bracket signal by the bridge, to the far right of the train is an early LMS wooden post signal.

Plate 143 (below): Class 25 No. 25184 hurries through Droitwich on the afternoon of 1st July 1983 with a Bescot to Severn Tunnel Junction freight train. On the left-hand side is an interesting GWR bracket signal with centre balanced arms.

Plate 142 (above): Class 47/4 No. 47532 pulls into Ulverston with the 16.23 Preston to Barrow train on a very wet 18th April 1984. With exceptions, most of the signalling in this area is of the modern upper quadrant variety. The diamond on the signal indicates track circuiting at that point.

Plate 144 (above): The 08.25 Newquay to Par train approaches St. Blazey on 27th April 1984. The signal on the left controls the line to St. Blazey yard, and the one on the right to the main line.

Plate 145 (above right): Class 207 'East Sussex' diesel electric unit No. 1310 approaches the LBSCR signal box at Birchden Junction with the 12.52 Tonbridge—Eridge service on 31st August 1983.

Plate 146 (right): Passing a lower quadrant bracket signal at Cowley Bridge Junction, on the evening of 29th July 1983, is Class 33/0 No. 33062 with an 'up' ballast train from Meldon Quarry.

Plate 147: Brundall Station is bathed in sunlight as Class 31 No. 31261 pulls through on Saturday 6th August 1983 and approaches the junction for the Lowestoft and Yarmouth lines with the 11.28 Norwich to Yarmouth train. Contrast the modern BR signal on the right with the signal on the left which has a GER post with LNER fitments. The guide marks on the post would seem to indicate that at one stage this was a lower quadrant signal.

Plate 148: A busy scene at Scarborough on Sunday, 14th August 1983, as Class 45 'Peak' No. 45023 *The Royal Pioneer Corps* pulls into the station with the 08.00 from Manchester (Victoria). Waiting to leave with the 11.00 service to Leeds is Class 47/0 No. 47212. The gantry is of NER origin with LNER type dolls.

Plate 149 (above): Class 37 No. 37262 pulls out of Achnasheen with the 09.30 (Sundays only) Inverness—Kyle of Lochalsh train, on 21st August 1983, and approaches a home and distant signal of LMS design.

Plate 150 (above right): The 06.00 Glasgow—Mallaig train hauled by Class 37 No. 37112 approaches Glenfinnan on 22nd August 1983. On the left of the train is a good example of a North British lattice post signal with LNER attachments, complete with an elegant finial. The box is also of North British origin to a basic Railway Signal Company design.

Plate 151 (right): Once again North British posts frame Class 37 No. 37112 as it arrives at Arisaig with the 16.30 Fort William to Mallaig train on 22nd August 1983.

Plate 152 (above): Class 50 No. 50023 *Howe* speeds past a modern three doll upper quadrant bracket signal at Langley, in the West Midlands, and heads for Birmingham with a football special from Plymouth on 14th April 1984.

Plate 153 (below): A pair of Class 50 locomotives, Nos. 50025 *Invincible* and 50004 *St. Vincent*, drift through Lostwithiel on the evening of 26th April 1984. They are on their way to Burngullow in order to work out an evening spoil train to Sittingbourne. The GWR bracket signal contrasts with the GWR type Sykes banner repeater signal.

Plate 154: GWR style lower quadrant signals are still in use on the North — West route, as can be seen in this picture of Class 33/0 No. 33029 leaving Craven Arms, on 28th January 1984, with the 13.25 Crewe—Cardiff train. The line in the foreground is part of the junction for the Central Wales line. Note also the ground frame.

Plate 155: Class 47/0 No. 47291 enters Bedale, on the morning of 16th April 1984, with the Tees Yard to Redmire empty hoppers. The North Eastern lower quadrant signal (with replacement finial) contrasts with the LNER upper quadrant.

Plate 156: Stabled at Exeter Depot on 28th April 1984 are Class 46 'Peak' No. 46028, Class 47 No. 47094 and an unidentified Class 45 'Peak'. Overlooking the scene is a typical GWR loop or siding signal, complete with route indicator.

Plate 157: Class 73 electro-diesel No. 73109 ambles into Hove Station at midday on 30th August 1983 with an 'up' pick-up goods, and approaches a Southern Railway two doll bracket signal, which is somewhat disfigured by the colour light signal.

Plate 158: On 16th July 1983, Class 45 'Peak' No. 45007 speeds through Havenhouse Station with the 08.25 (SO) Sheffield to Skegness train. The somersault signal protecting the crossing and the station buildings date from pre-grouping days and all are of GNR origin.

Plate 159 (left): In this picture, taken on 17th April 1984, we see the rear of the 16.42 Middlesbrough to Whitby train approaching Battersby Junction. It is passing an NER wooden slotted post fixed distant signal.

Plate 160 (below): Class 47/0 No. 47117 approaches Hellifield, from the Blackburn direction, on 15th April 1984. On the left is the line to Skipton. These splendid semaphores are fine examples of early LMS wooden post bracket signals, the actual brackets being to MR style with LMS fitments.

Plate 161 (right): A Class 45/1 'Peak' locomotive, No. 45137 *The Bedfordshire and Hertfordshire Regiment (T.A.),* leaves Skegness, on 16th July 1983, with the 13.00 (SO) train to Derby. In the background a Class 37 locomotive, No. 37196, waits to leave with the 13.20 service to Manchester (Piccadilly). The signal on the left is an LNER wooden post with miniature arm to control sidings and loops, and the signal next to it is a conversion from a GNR somersault signal.

Plate 162 (below): The 13.10 Westbury to Weymouth train, hauled by Class 47/0 No. 47147, speeds past a fine array of GWR semaphores at Castle Cary on 29th August 1983.

Plate 163 (above): Class 40 No. 40028 approaches an LMS three doll bracket signal at Mostyn Dock (North Wales) whilst in charge of the 11.15 Bangor to Manchester (Victoria) train on 18th June 1983.

Plate 164 (below): The NER signal box at Shildon overlooks Class 37 No. 37100 as it heads for Bishop Auckland with a coal train on 16th April 1984. A Class 31 locomotive waits to leave the yard on the left (which runs on into the BR workshops).

Plate 165 (above): Passing the former MR goods warehouse at Leicester (North), on 15th June 1983, is Class 45/1 'Peak' No. 45150 with the 08.50 Derby—St. Pancras service. The bracket signals are of LMS pattern.

Plate 166 (below): This well-known GWR gantry at Aller Junction gives 'road clear' to Class 46 'Peak' No. 46037 on a 'Saga' train to Plymouth, on 28th May 1984. As can also be seen there is a train due on the 'down' line to Paignton.

Plate 167 (above): The stations and surrounding lines of most large seaside towns in Britain seem to cling to semaphore signals, and the famous resort of Rhyl in North Wales is no exception. Passing under this fine gantry of wooden post LMS signals, at Rhyl, is Class 47/4 No. 47549 with the 10.10 Holyhead—Crewe working on 4th June 1983.

Plate 168 (below): Although Crediton was a former Southern Railway station the signals have now been changed to GWR lower quadrant style. In this view, taken on 31st July 1983, the driver of the 12.38 Barnstaple—Exeter is handing over the token to the signalman, for although there are two tracks in the Barnstaple direction, the line on the left is in fact to Meldon Quarry. Hauling the train is Class 33/0 No. 33062.

Plate 169 (above): Class 47/3 No. 47329 makes a fuss as it accelerates out of Taunton and passes under the GWR gantry with a down extra on 29th July 1983.

Plate 170 (below): The 14.25 service to Exmouth comprising two three car units and headed by Class 118 Birmingham RC&W unit No. P464, passes the LSWR box at Exeter (Central) Station on Sunday, 31st July 1983.

Plate 171 (above): Evening shunting at Lincoln by an unidentified Class 31 on 25th July 1983. The location is Sincil Junction, which still has an abundance of GNR and LNER signals.

Plate 172 (below): A busy scene at Norwich, on 6th August 1983, as Class 37 No. 37041 snakes out of Thorpe Station with the 09.24 (SO) to Liverpool Street. In the background is a Class 47 with the 09.40 to Liverpool Street. With the Eastern Region electrification scheme well under way, scenes like this will obviously soon disappear. The bracket signals are LNER, but the box dates back to GER days. The building in the top right-hand corner always amuses me; at first glance it looks like a giant face overlooking the station.

Plate 175 (above): With the city of Manchester in the background, Class 47/4 No. 47455 approaches the L&Y signal box at Miles Platting with the 13.25 to Scarborough on 6th January 1984. The bracket signal is of BR design.

Plate 173 (above left): What better place to find a Midland Railway wooden post signal with LMS fittings than on the Settle—Carlisle route. The location is the southern end of Blea Moor Tunnel, on 7th April 1984, and the train is a Hertford to Carlisle special.

Plate 174 (left): Class 37 No. 37262 drifts into Achnasheen with the 09.30 (SuO) Inverness—Kyle of Lochalsh train, on 21st August 1983. The splendid Highland Railway box and lattice post signal complete the scene.

Plate 176 (right): This fine Midland Railway box at Bradford (Forster Square) Station acts as a reminder of the station's former splendour. The local train leaving, on 4th November 1983, is the 15.00 service to Keighley.

Plate 177: The 16.45 Paddington—Plymouth HST service leaves Castle Cary on 7th May 1984. On the left is a GWR bracket signal (soon to be replaced), and the signal on the right is a GWR backing signal, complete with route indicator.

Plate 178: The late evening sun glints on the rear of the 19.59 Lowestoft to Norwich train as it leaves Lowestoft, on 5th August 1983, hauled by Class 37 No. 37019. Silhouetted is a fine pair of LNER bracket signals, the one on the right also has a disc signal.

Plate 179: Blackpool (North) Station, on the late evening of 16th September 1983, showing the centrepiece of the illuminations — the famous tower — framed in an early LMS bracket signal. Waiting to leave (just behind the bottom of the gantry post) is a local train to Manchester.